John's Gospel

EXPLORING THE SEVEN MIRACULOUS SIGNS

CWR

Keith Hacking

Published 2004 by CWR, Waverley Abbey House, Waverley Lane, Farnham,
Surrey GU9 8EP England. Registered Charity No. 294387.
Registered Limited Company No. 1990308. Reprinted 2010, 2012, 2016.

Laurence Housman's poem on page 10 is taken from Anthony P. Castle, *Quotes
and Anecdotes: The Essential Reference for Preachers & Teachers* (revised and
enlarged edition; Bury St. Edmunds: Kevin Mayhew, 1994), pp.212f.

For list of National Distributors, visit www.cwr.org.uk/distributors

Unless otherwise indicated, all Scripture references are from the Holy Bible:
New International Version (NIV), copyright © 1973, 1978, 1984 by the
International Bible Society.

Concept development, editing, design and production by CWR.
Front cover image: Roger Walker.
Printed in the UK by Linney Group

ISBN 978-1-85345-295-6

Contents

Introduction

Anyone reading the first three Gospels, Matthew, Mark and Luke, soon realises that miracles were a characteristic feature in the ministry of Jesus. In the fourth Gospel, John also tells us that Jesus performed many miracles that were witnessed by the disciples (John 20:30), but he says that he has deliberately chosen to include in his Gospel only seven of these miracles. Why is this? John gives us the answer in 20:31 where he says that the miracles which appear in his Gospel 'are written that you may believe that Jesus is the Christ, the Son of God, and that by believing you may have life in his name'.

The usual Greek word used for miracles in the New Testament is *dynamis* (pronounced dun-a-mis, and meaning literally 'deed of power') from which we get English words such as 'dynamic' and 'dynamite'. However, John is not content with just calling them 'miracles'. He uses another Greek word, *semion* (pronounced say-may-on) meaning 'sign'. In the Greek translation of the Old Testament, known as the Septuagint after the 70 Jewish scholars involved in its translation from Hebrew during the second century BC, the same Greek word for 'sign' occurs 125 times. An example of a sign in the Old Testament, which would be familiar to John's Jewish readers, would be the covenantal 'sign' of circumcision (Gen. 17:11). More notably, signs were associated with the Exodus when God used 'signs' performed through Moses to persuade Pharaoh to release the enslaved Israelites (Exod. 7:1–5; Psa. 78:43). Again, John's first readers would immediately make the connection between the signs performed by Jesus and God's saving activity in the Exodus.

In the first three Gospels, known collectively as the Synoptic Gospels because of the many parallel accounts they contain, Jesus performed no less than thirty-four miracles, not including parallel accounts of the same miracles. These 'deeds of power' are closely associated with Jesus' message about the presence of the kingdom of God. His miracles of healing, exorcism, feeding large crowds, walking on water, calming storms and even raising the dead, demonstrate in the most impressive ways that God's kingdom power is present in the ministry and message of His Messiah, Jesus.

In fact, miracles were such a distinctive feature of Jesus' ministry that when Peter was preaching to the crowds in Jerusalem at Pentecost and explaining how Joel's Old Testament prophecy is being fulfilled before their eyes, he described Jesus as 'a man accredited by God to you by miracles, wonders and signs, which God did among you through him' (Acts 2:22). Again, when Peter is preaching the gospel to the Gentile Cornelius and his household, he tells them how Jesus, anointed with the Holy Spirit and with power, went about healing people (Acts 10:38).

When the word 'sign' is used in the Synoptic Gospels it is in a negative way and associated with the unbelief of Jesus' opponents. They demand a sign from Him, which He refuses, telling them that the only sign they will receive is the 'sign of Jonah' (Matt. 12:38–39; Mark 8:11; Luke 11:16) – a reference to Jesus' resurrection. The word 'sign' is also used by Jesus as He looks forward prophetically to the end-times (Matt. 24:3,24,30). Judas' kiss of betrayal in Gethsemane is also called a 'sign' in the Greek text, although the NIV translates this as 'signal' (Matt. 26:48).

In John's Gospel the word 'sign' occurs seventeen times. Apart from specific signs, John also refers to Jesus' signs in a more general way without going into detail (see, for example, 2:23; 3:2; 6:2, 26; 7:31; 9:16; 11:47; 12:37). While John refers to Jesus' miracles as signs, Jesus Himself calls them His 'works'. In either case, their purpose is to lead to belief in Jesus and what He says about Himself. In selecting and recording particular signs from all the many miracles performed by Jesus and witnessed by the disciples, John's aim is to help his readers recognise Jesus' glory in them, in much the same way that the first followers of Jesus saw His glory revealed in the first miracle or sign He performed at the wedding in Cana – with the result that they 'put their faith in him' (John 2:11). To do this, John describes each of the selected signs in detail and then goes on to reveal to his readers the significance of each particular one.

The number of signs he chose would have particular significance for his first readers who would be aware that the number 'seven' was regarded as the perfect number, symbolising completeness. In Matthew's Gospel, when Peter asks how often he should forgive someone who offends him, he uses the perfect number, seven, to which Jesus replies that Christian forgiveness should go far beyond even such a complete number of occasions (Matt. 18:21f.).

As you will discover for yourself in these sessions, each of the signs in John has a special significance in the Gospel narrative. They allow us to glimpse Jesus' glory and they point forward to the saving work of the incarnate Christ. Over the next few weeks, as we dig deeper into the meaning and significance of the signs recorded by John may we too see more of Jesus' glory for ourselves and put our faith more firmly in Him.

WEEK 1

The Best is Yet to Come

Jesus changes water into wine

Opening Icebreaker

What is the most memorable thing that has happened
whilst you were attending a wedding? Share your
experience briefly with the group.

Bible Reading

- John 1:1–14; 2:1–11
- 2 Corinthians 5:16–21

Key Verse: 'And the Word became flesh and
lived among us, and we have seen his glory …'
(John 1:14, NRSV)

Focus: The revelation of the glory of Christ – John 1:14

Opening Our Eyes

In a striking poetic commentary on the prologue to John's Gospel, Laurence Housman writes:

Light looked down and beheld Darkness:
'Thither will I go,' said Light.
Peace looked down and beheld War:
'Thither will I go,' said Peace.
Love looked down and beheld Hatred:
'Thither will I go,' said Love.
So came Light and shone.
So came Peace and gave rest.
So came Love and brought life.
And the Word was made flesh and dwelt among us.

In both Jewish and Greek thinking there was the concept of the creative Word (Gk: *Logos*). In the story of creation in Genesis, God speaks and the universe is brought into being: And God said, let there be light, day, night, sky, land and sea … (Gen. 1:3–9). In the book of Proverbs, we read how Wisdom was brought into being by God before creation (Prov. 8:22–9:2). Wisdom says 'when he marked out the foundations of the earth, then I was beside him, like a master worker' (NRSV). For the Greeks, the *Logos* was responsible for holding together the ordered universe, for ensuring that the seasons came and went, the tides ebbed and flowed and the stars ran their course in the heavens.

In the Gospels of Matthew and Luke we read of the incarnation, the birth of the Child, Jesus. But John goes even further. In his prologue, he tells us that God's creative Word – God Himself – identified fully with humanity by becoming a human being residing at a particular time and in a particular geographical location. Before John even begins to tell us about the earthly ministry of Jesus, he establishes for his readers, in the most profound way, the heavenly identity of the Man, Jesus of Nazareth, the son of Joseph (1:45).

Following John the Baptist's testimony – when he calls Jesus the Lamb of God, in a clear reference to the sacrificial way in which His earthly ministry will end in crucifixion and death (1:29–35) – He begins to attract a small circle of disciples. Within the context of the narrative, John's readers are also made aware that the Spirit of God is with Jesus in the fullest possible way (1:32), that Jesus is, in fact, the Son of God (1:34).

Importantly here, John also alerts us to the conflict that will arise out of Jesus' mission and the claims He makes about Himself throughout the Gospel. During a conversation with Him, Nathanael misinterprets Jesus' identity. He says, 'Rabbi, you are the Son of God', immediately interpreting that in political terms –'you are the King of Israel' (1:43–50; cf. 6:15). Jesus corrects him by referring to Himself rather as the Son of Man (1:51), the heavenly figure associated in Jewish thinking with the end-time (cf. Mark 13:1–27).

And so we arrive at the opening scene of the first of Jesus' seven signs, where He changes water into wine at the wedding He is attending with His mother and His disciples at Cana.

Discussion Starters

1. Why do you think Jesus and His disciples went to the wedding?

_____

_____

_____

_____

2. So far in John's Gospel, Jesus has not performed any miracles. Why do you think Jesus' mother now involves Him when the wine runs out?

_____

_____

_____

_____

3. How does this first sign relate to Jesus' response to His mother (cf. 7:6, 8, 30; 8:20; 12:23; 13:1; 17:1)?

_____

_____

_____

_____

4. Given the capacity of the ceremonial washing jars used, what does this tell us about the nature of God's provision?

_____

_____

_____

_____

5. What do you think is the significance of the master of the banquet's comparison in the quality of the wine?

_____

_____

_____

_____

_____

6. Can you think of a specific instance when God provided for you that you would like to share with the group?

_____

_____

_____

_____

7. How do you think this story links back to the prologue (John 1:1–14)?

_____

_____

_____

_____

8. Why do you think John chose this particular miracle to be the first of the seven signs he records in his Gospel?

_____

_____

_____

_____

9. What does this sign tell us about Jesus' glory, and how does it help us, like the disciples, to put our faith in Him?

_____

_____

_____

_____

Personal Application

After performing His first 'sign' at the wedding in Cana, Jesus' disciples are able to regard Him in a different light. Their relationship with Jesus has been enriched because they have glimpsed something more of the truth of who He really is and the result, John tells us, is that they 'put their faith in him' (John 2:11). A similar pattern can often be reflected in our Christian experience today. We begin to follow Jesus – often on the strength of what someone has told us (cf. John 1:40–42) – which is in itself a leap of faith. But, like any personal relationship, it is often only when we begin to glimpse for ourselves the truth of who Jesus really is, as He reveals His glory to us in a personal way, that we begin to put our trust and confidence in Him.

Seeing Jesus in the Scriptures

The opening words of John's Gospel (John 1:1–14) are some of the most profound words ever written. 'In the beginning …' calls to mind God's creative activity in Genesis 1:1. John tells us that the Word (Gk: *Logos*) was with God in the beginning (1:1) and the Word was God and yet mysteriously shared fellowship with God (1:2) and was instrumental in creation (1:3). The greatest miracle of all is that God's creative Word became a human being and lived in space and time amongst ordinary people. Jesus the incarnate Son of God was not only the mediator of creation, but is also the mediator of our new creation 'in Christ' (2 Cor. 5:17). Jesus, full of grace and truth, reflects for us God's true character, and in recognising this we see His glory (1:14).

WEEK 2

God's Timing is Perfect

An official's son is healed

Opening Icebreaker

Recall the most serious illness or injury either you or a member of your family had as a child. What were your feelings at the time?

Bible Reading

- John 4:1–54
- Matthew 8:5–13
- Romans 5:6–11

Key Verse: 'Then the father realised that this was the exact time at which Jesus had said to him, "Your son will live." So he and all his household believed.' (John 4:53)

Focus: God's perfect timing

Opening Our Eyes

After performing the first miracle at the wedding in Cana, Jesus travelled up to Jerusalem for Passover. What must His disciples have felt when they saw Him overturning the money-changers' tables and driving out the sacrificial animals from the Temple courts? Having glimpsed Jesus' glory through that first 'sign', they were in the right frame of mind to recall and apply Scripture to His shocking actions (2.17; cf. Psa. 69:9).

The reaction of Jewish observers, however, would have been outrage, and so they demanded of Him a further sign (2:18) to prove that He possessed the heavenly authority to act as He did. Jesus' response is enigmatic and, in retrospect, His disciples realise that He was pointing them forward to His death and resurrection (2:19–22). Although John often mentions Jesus being in the Temple, he makes no subsequent mention of Jesus' response here (in 2:19) at His trial. However, we know from the other Gospels that this was used against Jesus then by His Jewish accusers (Matt. 26:59–61; Mark 14:57–58).

Jesus continued to teach and perform miracles in Jerusalem during the period of Passover, with the result that at least some of those who saw His miracles believed in Him. But their belief seems to have been rather questionable; John tells us that Jesus' knowledge of human nature allowed Him to see the fickleness of their faith at this point (2:24; cf. 6:15).

In chapter 3, John relates the story of Jesus' meeting with Nicodemus where Jesus again alludes to His death on the cross (3:14). This is followed by the most succinct expression of the Christian gospel in the whole of the New Testament, 'For God so loved the world that he gave his one and only Son, that whoever believes in him shall not perish but have eternal life' (3:16).

After this, Jesus and His disciples spent some time in the Judean countryside, where John the Baptist gave further testimony about Jesus (3:25–36). On the way back to Galilee they passed through Samaria where, we are told, many Samaritans believed in Him – and not just because of the Samaritan woman's testimony but because of their personal experience of Jesus (4:42).

After leaving Samaria Jesus is welcomed back to Cana in Galilee by the people because they too had gone up to Jerusalem for the Passover and had witnessed the other signs He had performed. While there, He is approached by a royal official in the service of King Herod Antipas, whose son is seriously ill. In response to the man's request, Jesus performs a second miraculous sign, this time, significantly, at a distance, which also leads to faith and which reveals for us insights into God's perfect timing.

Discussion Starters

1. Look at what Jesus is reported having said in verse 44. Has there been a time in your life when you felt rejected because of your Christian faith?

_____

_____

_____

_____

2. Looking back to John 2:11 and at 20:30–31, how do you account for Jesus' comment in verse 48?

_____

_____

_____

_____

3. What do you think should be our attitude to signs and wonders today?

_____

_____

_____

_____

4. Have you experienced the miraculous in your life? What effect does this have on your life today?

_____

_____

_____

_____

5. What does the royal official's travelling from Capernaum to Cana tell us about (a) the royal official and (b) Jesus?

_____

_____

_____

_____

6. Putting yourself in the place of the official who is desperately worried about his son, how would you react to Jesus' response?

_____

_____

_____

_____

7. What are the most dramatic circumstances in which you have had to exercise faith? How did God work in them?

_____

_____

_____

_____

8. What does this incident teach us about God's timing? Can you give an example of God's timing at work in your own life?

_____

_____

_____

_____

9. What effect has your becoming a Christian had on your family and friends?

_____

_____

_____

_____

Personal Application

How often do we all allow our actions to be dictated by our peers? We dress, act, speak and even think in particular ways because this allows us to feel accepted by the crowd. When we take our Christian commitment seriously, this often brings us into conflict with the way in which society thinks and acts on important issues. As Christians, our supreme model is Jesus who always operated in a different way to the mindset of His day. When He made public His manifesto for mission in the synagogue in Nazareth He declared: 'The Spirit of the Lord is on me, because he has anointed me to preach good news to the poor. He has sent me to proclaim freedom for the prisoners and recovery of sight for the blind, to release the oppressed, to proclaim the year of the Lord's favour' (Luke 4:18f.).

Seeing Jesus in the Scriptures

When the royal official, clearly a man of high social standing, approaches Jesus, the former carpenter turned itinerant preacher, desperately seeking a cure for his sick child, Jesus refuses to 'play to the gallery'. He nevertheless has compassion for the man and says simply, 'You may go. Your son will live.' When the official returns home and finds his son well on the way to recovery he also discovers that at the very time Jesus gave the man His word that the boy would live was the point at which the fever left him. Jesus' integrity and God's perfect timing in the healing of the child had a life-changing impact on the official and his family.

WEEK 3

Healing and Wholeness

Healing at the pool

Opening Icebreaker

What are your favourite excuses for putting off things you know you ought to do? Give one example.

Bible Reading

• John 5:1–30

Key Verse: 'Do you want to become whole?'
(John 5:6, my translation)

Focus: Life through the Son (John 5:24)

Opening Our Eyes

As we reach chapter 5, we can see that John is beginning to establish a pattern in his narrative, with Jesus returning to Jerusalem to be present with the crowds during important feasts. In New Testament times there were three major feasts which Jews were encouraged to celebrate in Jerusalem: Passover, Pentecost and Tabernacles.

Passover, or the Feast of Unleavened Bread, commemorates
Israel's deliverance by God from slavery in Egypt (Exod. 23:15). It was celebrated on the fourteenth day of Nisan, the first month in the Jewish religious calendar (March/April, Lev. 23:5). For the seven days of the festival, unleavened bread was eaten, and on the first and last days sacrifices were offered in the Temple in Jerusalem, attended by hundreds, if not thousands, of Jews from Palestine and the Jewish *diaspora* scattered around the Roman Empire.

Pentecost, also known as the 'Feast of Weeks/Harvest' or, alternatively, 'day of firstfruits' (Exod. 23:16; 34:22; Num. 28:26; cf. Acts 2:1), was so called because it was celebrated fifty days from the beginning of Passover, and was also celebrated with sacrifices.

The third major feast, known as Tabernacles or Booths, was also known as the 'Feast of Ingathering' and celebrated God's provision in the harvest (Exod. 23:16; 34:22; Lev. 23:34; Deut. 16:13). This feast was celebrated in September/October over seven days when the people lived outside in makeshift booths made of branches and leaves from trees.

In chapter 2, John tells us that Jesus went up to Jerusalem at the time of Passover, and then in chapter 7 that He returns again to Jerusalem, this time during the autumn, for the Feast of Tabernacles. Here at the beginning of chapter 5, we learn that sometime after Jesus healed the royal official's son at Cana in Galilee, He returned to Jerusalem, again for a festival, which John does not identify on this occasion.

Once again water plays an important part in the narrative. At Cana, Jesus had turned water into wine and in chapter 4 during His conversation with a Samaritan woman at the well at Sychar, He turned the conversation about ordinary well-water into a conversation about 'water', which symbolically represents the eternal life which is available through God's Messiah, Jesus (4:13–26).

Now at the pool of Bethesda, water plays a central role in the narrative. The name 'Bethesda' is mentioned in the Dead Sea scrolls and, with its five porticos, archaeologists have excavated this double-pool just north of the Temple Mount and today it can be seen by visitors to Jerusalem. At the time of Jesus, Bethesda was known for its healing waters, rather like present-day Lourdes in France. The sick were brought to the pool in the belief that the waters held healing properties. Some old manuscripts speak of an angel of the Lord who stirred up the waters, indicating that healing was available to the sick (see verse 7). However, the oldest and best manuscripts do not contain this reference to the angel which is why verse 4 is missing from the majority of modern translations.

Unlike the previous two signs, following this miracle there is an extended monologue by Jesus through which John's readers gain new insight into just who Jesus really is in light of the absolutely stunning claim made by John in his prologue. God's creative Word, who was with God in the beginning, has been sent into the world to bring eternal life (5:24).

Discussion Starters

1. Imagine you are present at the pool of Bethesda. Describe the atmosphere, the smell and the noise. Share with the group how you would feel in a place like this.

_____

_____

_____

_____

2. What do you think Jesus means by His question to the invalid in verse 6? How would you describe the invalid's response?

_____

_____

_____

_____

3. If Jesus asked you if you wanted Him to make you well or 'whole', how would His question apply to you, and how would you respond?

_____

_____

_____

_____

4. In verse 14, Jesus tells the man, 'Stop sinning or something worse may happen to you.' How do you understand this in the context of the story? Would you agree with someone who said that all illness is the result of sin? If not, why not?

_____

_____

_____

_____

5. John tells us that this miraculous healing took place on the Sabbath (v.9b). What do you think of the reaction of the Jews? Have there been times in your own experience when your joy in the Lord has been affected negatively because of someone's concern over religious traditions?

_____

_____

_____

_____

6. In what ways is Jesus equal with the Father, and how does this relate to John 1:1, 14, 18?

_____

_____

_____

_____

7. How would you put verse 24 into your own words? How is this true for you?

_____

_____

_____

_____

8. How do people you know look for 'wholeness' outside of Christ?

_____

_____

_____

_____

9. In what ways can Jesus' accusation in verse 39 be true for Christians today? What should we do about it?

_____

_____

_____

_____

Personal Application

This third sign performed by Jesus, and His words which follow, present us with a challenge which encapsulates the good news for us today. Whoever we are, we have all experienced the bitterness of failure in our lives. This sense of failure can be most acute in our personal lives – in our relationships with others, and especially in our relationship with our innermost self. The lesson we learn here is that Jesus offers each and every one of us a second chance. If we are willing to hear, He asks us the same question that He asked the lame man two millennia ago, 'Do you want to become whole? Do you want a second chance?' To have the courage to admit our need and to take Jesus at His word is not to claim 'cheap grace'. The cost to our heavenly Father and His Son was enormous (cf. John 3:16).

Seeing Jesus in the Scriptures

The area of theology that is concerned with the Person and work of Jesus is called Christology, and this is a subject of primary concern for John throughout his Gospel. When Jesus is accused of making Himself equal with God because He called God His Father (5:17), we learn from His response that His earthly mission is so bound up with the will of His Father that who He is and what He does truly reflects the will of God (5:19). Jesus does not seek to please Himself, but the Father who sent Him and from whom He receives authority (5:27,30). Just as the Father raises the dead, so too Jesus, as the Son of God, gives life (5:21) and, as the Son of Man, has authority from the Father to judge the world (5:27f.).

WEEK 4

Jesus and the Unexpected

Feeding the five thousand
Jesus walks on the water

Opening Icebreaker

If your income were suddenly doubled, how would you use the extra money?

Bible Reading

- John 6:1–21; 25–65
- Mark 6:30–44
- Deuteronomy 18:15–18

Key Verse: 'It is I; don't be afraid.' (John 6:20)

Focus: Jesus meets our needs – John 6:11

Opening Our Eyes

Chapter 6 falls into two parts; in the first, John records two miraculous signs: the feeding of the five thousand (6:1–15) followed by Jesus walking on the water (6:16–24). In the second part we have an important dialogue where Jesus describes Himself as the 'bread of life' (6:25–59). The chapter ends with a sifting of Jesus' followers, many of whom desert Him (6:60–71).

Feeding the multitude (6:1–15)
The famous missionary doctor and theologian, Albert Schweitzer, once said: 'The purpose of human life is to serve and to show compassion and the will to help others.' In this particular sign, Jesus provides us with an example *par excellence* of what Schweitzer meant.

Jesus is followed by a large crowd who are looking to see yet more miraculous healings, and on a mountainside, which would act as a natural amphitheatre, He sits down with His disciples in true rabbinic fashion (cf. Matt. 5:1). John tells us that this is around the time of Passover, which means that it must be either six or ten months after the festival noted in chapter 5, depending on whether this unnamed festival was Tabernacles or Pentecost.

Out of compassion for the crowd, Jesus uses five barley loaves and two fish and with these limited provisions miraculously feeds the crowd, distributing personally first the bread and then the fish, Himself. The people begin to speculate about who Jesus might be.

Here we have a conflation of contemporary Messianic ideas associated with the expectation of another prophet like Moses (Deut. 18:15–18), the expectation that Elijah will return (cf. John 1:19–20), and Jewish political aspirations which looked for a Davidic Messiah who would free Israel from foreign occupation. Realising that

the crowd were about to force their own expectations
on Him, and possibly embroil Him in an insurrection,
John tells us that Jesus withdrew to the mountain alone
(cf. Mark 6:46).

Walking on the water (6:16–24)
As the disciples set sail, they must have been filled with
mixed feelings. They, too, were Jews who would, no
doubt, share the popular Messianic expectations of the
crowd. What did the sign of the feeding of the crowd
in the wilderness really mean?

As they are pondering these things, conditions on the
Sea of Galilee suddenly change, as they still do today, and
the disciples find themselves having to row for the shore.
They must have been near exhaustion, having rowed over
three miles when, unbelievably, they encounter Jesus
walking towards them across the lake.

Some older commentators have tried to rationalise this
miracle, which is also recorded in Matthew and Mark
(Matt. 14:22–33; Mark 6:47–51) by suggesting that Jesus
only walked beside the sea. However, the Greek text
is clear that the disciples saw Jesus literally 'walking on
the sea and drawing near to the boat' (6:19, NRSV).

The disciples' response is, quite naturally, one of fear.
According to Matthew and Mark (Matt. 14:26; Mark 6:49)
the disciples think they are seeing a ghost, but here Jesus
reassures them by revealing His identity, 'It is I; don't
be afraid' (John 6:20). With these words, the disciples
overcome their fear and are then willing to take Jesus
into the boat. Coinciding with their willingness to receive
Jesus, they find themselves safely at their destination.
How often do we fail to recognise the presence of Jesus
in the middle of life's difficulties? What a privilege when
we receive some token of reassurance from the Lord:
'Don't be afraid, it is I.'

Discussion Starters

1. Why do the crowd follow Jesus? How is this reflected in the Church today?

2. Bearing in mind Jesus' miracle at the wedding in Cana, in what way, do you think, was Jesus seeking to test Philip (6:5ff)? Are you sometimes like Philip and Andrew; if so, how?

3. What evidence is there that this sign may have a sacramental theme? In other words, do you think John has in mind here the sharing of bread at the celebration of communion and if so what is there in the passage that makes you think so?

4. Which Old Testament character is brought to mind through Jesus' actions here? Why?

5. John tells us that there was more food left over after the feeding than there had been to start with – how do you understand this? What is your experience of God's provision?

_____

_____

_____

_____

6. Imagining yourself as one of the rowers in the boat (6:16–24), how would you have reacted if you had seen Jesus walking towards you across the sea?

_____

_____

_____

_____

7. Seeing Jesus under these circumstances reminded the disciples, who were Jesus' constant companions, to have regard for His heavenly status. How do you think this might affect the way we regard our personal relationship with Him?

_____

_____

_____

_____

8. How does being a Christian affect the way you react to storms in your life?

_____

_____

_____

_____

9. How do you understand verse 21, and how would you apply this to your own experience?

_____

_____

_____

_____

Personal Application

George Muller, who in the nineteenth century famously ran an orphanage in Bristol living entirely on faith, recording his experience of God's daily provision in his journal, once wrote: 'The beginning of anxiety is the end of faith, and the beginning of true faith is the end of anxiety.' Muller's wonderful insight into the providence of God summarises the message for us in these two signs – the miraculous feeding and Jesus walking on the water. My family motto is *Dominus Providebit* – God provides – how true this has been in my own Christian life. May it also be true in your experience.

Seeing Jesus in the Scriptures

In the case of both of the signs we have looked at in this session, we find Jesus generously meeting the needs of those who look to Him. In the case of the crowd who had followed Him to a remote Galilean shore, Jesus meets their physical needs when in human terms the available resources appear wholly inadequate. Jesus' provision is so abundant that there is more than enough for everyone.

In the case of the beleaguered disciples rowing for their lives, even though they had failed to grasp the signifi-cance of the feeding miracle, Jesus meets their need for reassurance by revealing His mastery over the elements. Once they had mustered the courage to accept Jesus as He appeared to them in this situation, they find that the reason for their panic has subsided and they arrive at their destination.

WEEK 5

Living Bread

Jesus the bread of life

Opening Icebreaker

What is your favourite kind of bread, and how do you like to eat it?

Bible Reading

- John 6:25–70
- Exodus 16:1–35

Key Verse: 'I am the living bread that came down from heaven. If anyone eats of this bread, he will live forever. This bread is my flesh, which I will give for the life of the world.' (John 6:51)

Focus: Jesus the bread of life (John 6:48)

Opening Our Eyes

A man walking along a railway track in central India came across some scraps of paper. Picking up one of them, he read in his own language the words, 'I am the bread of life'. When he reached his destination he asked a friend if he knew where the words came from and was told that they were from the Christian Scriptures. The words continued to haunt him and he obtained a copy of the New Testament written in his own language from a Christian missionary who explained that they were the words of Jesus. After reading the gospel story, the man's heart was set on fire for Christ and he became an itinerant Christian preacher travelling throughout his province in central India. Jesus had truly become the bread of life for that man.

The crowd, who had witnessed the sign of the miraculous feeding the day before, now follow Jesus to Capernaum, and the ensuing dialogue takes place in the local synagogue (v.59). He refuses their request for yet another sign, and bases His teaching on an exposition of the Old Testament miracle of the manna from heaven. The source for the quotation in verse 31 is unclear; it may be a conflation of ideas found in Nehemiah 9:15 and Psalm 78:24. Jesus' exposition falls into three parts.

John 6:32–40: Jesus takes the first part of the text in Nehemiah He 'gave them bread from heaven …' The manna which God supplied to Israel in the wilderness may be understood as a 'type', which foreshadowed the coming of Jesus, the true bread. To receive this bread is to receive eternal life for all who believe in Him.

John 6:41–51: Jesus' exposition moves to the second part of the quotation: '… bread from heaven to eat'. Jesus is the living bread of life sent from heaven and the 'bread' of His flesh is given for the world. The manna eaten in the wilderness sustained life only in a temporary way. Jesus, as the living bread, has come down from heaven in order to give Himself for the life of the world. Those who participate in Him will be sustained in an eternal way.

John 6:52–58: Finally, there is an exposition of what it means 'to eat' Jesus' flesh and drink His blood. In the eucharistic language used here by Jesus, we have a foreshadowing of the Last Supper and His coming death on the cross. The metaphor has shifted from Jesus as the 'bread of life' to His 'flesh' and His 'blood'. The urgency increases: unless we eat His 'flesh' and drink His 'blood', we have no 'life' in us. But the relationship between Christ and the believer who 'eats' will be sustained into eternity. As the Son lives through the Father, so the believer can have eternal life only through the Son.

Many of Jesus' listeners find His claims unacceptable and cease to follow Him. How often today do we find the teaching of the New Testament about the claims of Jesus being watered down in order not to give offence? Do we also stop following Jesus in some way because it has become politically incorrect? Or, with Peter, do we say, 'Lord, to whom shall we go? You have the words of eternal life. We believe and know that you are the Holy One of God' (v.68)?

Discussion Starters

1. How does Jesus' response to the crowd, who have followed Him to Capernaum, illuminate the difference between His priorities and those of the crowd?

_____

_____

_____

_____

_____

2. Describe your daily spiritual practice. How do you find this helps you to adjust your priorities so that they better reflect God's priorities as revealed in Scripture?

_____

_____

_____

_____

_____

3. In what ways do the claims Jesus makes in verses 35–40 go beyond the typology or foreshadowing of the manna supplied by God in the wilderness?

_____

_____

_____

_____

_____

4. What part does the Father play in pointing people towards Jesus? What has been your experience of being drawn towards Him?

_____

_____

_____

_____

_____

5. Looking at verses 41–50, again in what ways do the claims of Jesus go beyond the typology of the manna?

_____

_____

_____

_____

_____

6. How do you understand Jesus' 'eucharistic' language in verses 51–58? How important for you are the eucharistic practices of the church you attend?

_____

_____

_____

_____

_____

7. John tells us that many of Jesus' disciples ceased to follow Him. Why is this? What does Peter recognise about Jesus that makes him want to remain a disciple?

_____

_____

_____

_____

8. How are the attitudes of Peter and/or those who cease to follow Jesus reflected in your experience?

_____

_____

_____

_____

Personal Application

Bishop Stephen Neill once said: 'Life is filled with meaning as soon as Jesus Christ enters into it.' How true this is. Jesus' claim to be the 'bread of life' (6:48) indicates that the kind of relationship God seeks to have with us in Christ is so close, so intimate, that it is like eating and drinking. In Middle Eastern society taking meals together is considered one of the most intimate forms of fellowship. It is intimate fellowship that Jesus desires with us and, at least in this sense, He becomes food and drink to us through the Holy Spirit.

Seeing Jesus in the Scriptures

Our focus this week is 'Jesus the bread of life' (John 6:48). When we look at the extended dialogue following the two miraculous signs, we find further clues about Jesus' true identity. In a clear reference to the Jewish law (6:28) Jesus points to Himself and His authoritative commission from the Father (6:29).

Jesus makes a number of further revelations about Himself. He has come down from heaven and is the 'bread' of God to which, typologically, the manna in the wilderness pointed. Food and water sustain physical life, but those who turn to Christ will be sustained in an eternal way. What is more, unlike the Jewish Law which excluded various kinds of people from full participation in the religious life of Israel, no one who turns to Christ will be turned away.

WEEK 6

Amazing Grace

Jesus heals a man born blind

Opening Icebreaker

Describe briefly any character traits you have inherited from your parents. As you grow older, are any of these becoming more dominant?

Bible Reading

- John 9:1–41
- Genesis 3:1–24

Key Verse: 'I was blind but now I see!' (John 9:25)

Focus: Amazing grace

Opening Our Eyes

In the first three Gospels there are several occasions on which we are told that Jesus' actions on the Sabbath gave rise to controversy and heated debate with His opponents. On this occasion, so far as Jesus' Pharisaic opponents were concerned, His using spittle to make clay constituted breaking the Sabbath prohibition on work, and healing on the Sabbath, unless a person was in mortal danger which was not the case here, was also not allowed.

Jesus succinctly summarised His attitude to His opponents' objections when He said: 'The Sabbath was made for man, not man for the Sabbath' (Mark 2:27). In John's Gospel, there are three occasions when Jesus opposes hypocritical attitudes connected with keeping the Sabbath: the healing of the man at the pool of Bethesda (chap.5), during the Feast of Tabernacles in Jerusalem (chap.7) and here in chapter 9.

That Father of the Reformation, John Calvin, once wrote: 'There is no greater darkness than ignorance of God.' The truth of this statement is revealed here in the attitude of the Pharisees who oppose Jesus. The Christian doctrine of original sin is concerned with articulating the reason for mankind's alienation from God and providing a starting point for salvation-history (cf. Gen. 3:16). The rabbis believed that the serpent in the story injected a poison into Eve, the mother of mankind, which was then passed on to her descendants. For the rabbis, the antidote to the poison of inherited sin was to be found in keeping the Law.

Also we find in the Old Testament the popular belief that the sins of parents would have negative consequences for their children, 'The fathers eat sour grapes, and the children's teeth are set on edge' (Jer. 31:29; Ezek. 18:2).

On both occasions in the Old Testament when this saying is quoted God makes it clear that He holds individuals responsible for their own wrongdoing.

Nevertheless, as John 9:1–3 makes clear, these superstitious ideas about sin and physical disability were still current in the first century, and Jesus' disciples appear to have been influenced by them when they ask, 'Rabbi, who sinned, this man or his parents, that he was born blind?' The Discussion Starters for this session will give an opportunity to discuss this further.

As the Pharisees investigate the healing, the man's parents are concerned that they will become victims of the Pharisees' opposition to Jesus, and be excluded from the synagogue. How easy it is to judge them, but how hard it can be to experience rejection and exclusion from a peer group. Their fear is clearly not without foundation, for when their son is called before the Pharisees a second time, and he defends Jesus against their arguments, the Pharisees throw him out, presumably excluding him from the synagogue (9:22, 34b; cf. 12:42; 16:2).

When Jesus hears about this He seeks out the man and reveals to him the truth about Himself. This results in the man coming to faith in the One who has opened His eyes physically and who cures him of spiritual blindness. Not content to let things rest, some Pharisees try to provoke Jesus with their questions, 'Are we blind too?' (9:40). Jesus' response cuts to the heart of the matter. The fact that they have set themselves up as beacons of light for others, and the more they enjoy a privileged position within their society because of it, the more harshly they will be judged themselves.

Discussion Starters

1. What view of suffering is expressed by the disciples? Why do you think Jesus rejects this explanation for the blind man's condition?

_____

_____

_____

_____

2. What are the different reactions to the healing of the blind man? Who does Jesus think is really blind?

_____

_____

_____

_____

3. Has any experience of illness or infirmity brought you closer to God?

_____

_____

_____

_____

4. In John 9:16, on the basis of their view of His religious practice, the Pharisees deny that Jesus is from God. Are there things you will not do on Sundays?

_____

_____

_____

_____

5. Name some of the things that divide Christians.

_____

_____

_____

_____

6. Do you ever feel threatened by Christians whose beliefs and practices are different from those of your own Christian tradition?

_____

_____

_____

_____

7. Has following Jesus ever led to your being excluded from any group? How did you feel?

_____

_____

_____

_____

8. What is it about the former blind man's present circumstances that cause Jesus to seek him out? Why do you think Jesus waits until this point to reveal the truth about Himself?

_____

_____

_____

_____

9. What does this teach us about evangelism?

_____

_____

_____

_____

10. What does Jesus' condemnation of the Pharisees (v.41) teach us about being the people of God?

_____

_____

_____

_____

Personal Application

The healed man's response to the grace of Jesus provides us with a wonderful example of what can happen as we respond positively to the claims of Christ. The man born blind receives not only physical healing but also the opening of his spiritual eyes to see the truth of God's salvation in Christ. This was certainly also the experience of the former slave trader, John Newton, who wrote in his famous hymn, 'Amazing Grace': 'I once was lost, but now am found, was blind, but now I see.' Over the next week, reflect on the ways in which you find you can identify with both the experience of the blind man and that reflected in John Newton's words.

Seeing Jesus in the Scriptures

There are three stages to the structure of chapter 9 that reveal deeper and deeper truths about Jesus – almost like a three-point sermon! In stage one, Jesus is called simply a man (9:11). In the incarnation, the Word became flesh and lived amongst us as the Man, Jesus of Nazareth (John 1:14). In stage two, Jesus is recognised as a prophet (9:17) because of the miraculous healing sign which would call to mind the Old Testament connection between signs and the prophets (Exod. 4:1–17; cf. 18:15). Finally, in stage three, Jesus is recognised as the Son of Man who will judge the world. The only appropriate response is to worship Him (9:35, 38).

WEEK 7

Death Loses its Sting

Jesus raises Lazarus from the dead

Opening Icebreaker

Is there an incident that stands out in your memory where you feel you were let down by your best friend?

Bible Reading

- John 11:1–44
- 1 Corinthians 15:1–58

Key Verse: 'I am the resurrection and the life. He who believes in me will live, even though he dies; and whoever lives and believes in me will never die.' (John 11:25–26)

Focus: Resurrection life in Christ

Opening Our Eyes

The nineteenth-century German philosopher, Arthur Schopenhauer, once said: 'Every parting gives a foretaste of death; every coming together again a foretaste of the resurrection.' This is certainly true of the story of the raising of Lazarus from the dead, the seventh of Jesus' miraculous signs chosen by John for inclusion in his Gospel. All the drama of death, so familiar to those of us who have lost a family member or friend, is shared here by Jesus.

The previous chapter ends with an attempt to seize Jesus (10:39), but He escapes, leaves Jerusalem and returns to the wilderness where John the Baptist used to baptise on the banks of the Jordan – the very place where Jesus had first been commissioned for public ministry by His heavenly Father (10:40; cf. Luke 3:21–22). Was this just nostalgia on Jesus' part, or was He returning to a place of special significance for Him, in order to be strengthened for what lay ahead?

Whatever Jesus' reason for choosing this location, even though John tells us it was winter (10:22), the crowds continued to seek him out. Perhaps they too were touched by this special place which reminded them of John the Baptist, and also caused them to recall the signs that Jesus had performed. In making the contrast between Jesus and His forerunner, they came to realise the truth of what John had said about Jesus, and this led them to believe in Him (10:42).

The scene is now set for John to recount the incidents surrounding the seventh and final sign he has chosen. By the time we come to the story of Lazarus, we are already aware that Jesus is inextricably in conflict with the Jewish authorities. Yet the common people continue to follow

Him from place to place wanting to believe that He is truly from God.

The raising of Lazarus creates two opposing effects in the narrative. On the one hand, it results in many who witness this most extraordinary miracle putting their faith in Jesus. He has just confirmed for them that He must truly be from God, and in the sign has revealed for them something of God's own glory (11:40, 42).

On the other hand, the reaction of the authorities in Jerusalem is entirely different. They are prepared to admit that Jesus really is performing some remarkable miracles that, according to their own stated beliefs, are evidence of God's validation of His message. Indeed, they foresee that, as a result, the whole country will come to believe in Him. Nevertheless, they think only of self-preservation and the threat to their own position of leadership which they believe may be brought to an end by the occupying Romans, as a result of an insurrection inspired by the Messianic expectations of the people.

And so, with this seventh sign, we reach a turning point in the Gospel narrative marked by John's chilling comment: 'So from that day on they plotted to take his life' (11:53).

Discussion Starters

1. Given the close relationship that existed between Jesus and Lazarus' family, how do you account for Jesus' deliberate delay?

_____

_____

_____

_____

2. How does Jesus' use of the metaphor, 'sleep', for death create a point of contact between this incident and attitudes to death in our own society?

_____

_____

_____

_____

3. What do Jesus' conversations, first with Martha and then with Mary, reveal about His relationship with the two women (cf. Luke 10:38–42; John 12:1–3)?

_____

_____

_____

_____

4. When did you last say, 'If only ...'?

_____

_____

_____

_____

5. Which of the two women symbolises your own relationship with Jesus, and why? How do you feel about this?

_____

_____

_____

_____

_____

_____

6. Do you think John intends us to understand the raising of Lazarus as a resurrection from the dead (cf. Matt. 28:5f.); resuscitation from the dead; a foreshadowing of Jesus' forthcoming resurrection?

_____

_____

_____

_____

7. How are we to understand the resurrection in the light of Jesus' seemingly contradictory statements about living and dying in verse 25b?

_____

_____

_____

_____

8. How does this seventh sign fulfil John's criteria for inclusion in his Gospel (20:30f.)?

_____

_____

_____

_____

9. It has been said that the first three Gospels tell the story of the life of Jesus, and that John's is a meditation on the *meaning* of Jesus' life. Having spent the past seven sessions studying John's Gospel, what do you think?

_____

_____

_____

_____

Personal Application

Read again John's statement in 3:16 and think about how the cost of resurrection-life in Christ applies to your relationships on a day-to-day basis – at home and work? Now read John 10:10. Consider the alternatives which are available to inform all of us on a daily basis, resolving to claim Jesus' promise of fullness of life.

Seeing Jesus in the Scriptures

The outstanding claim made by Jesus during the telling of incidents surrounding the raising of Lazarus is in verses 25–26 where He says: 'I am the resurrection and the life. He who believes in me will live, even though he dies; and whoever lives and believes in me will never die.' It is here that we reach the very heart of the Christian message.

In his discussion of the resurrection state in his first letter to the Christians in Corinth, Paul makes the point that 'if Christ has not been raised, your faith is futile; you are still in your sins … But Christ has indeed been raised from the dead, the firstfruits of those who have fallen asleep' (1 Cor. 15:17–20).

Jesus' claim to be 'the resurrection and the life' may be understood as affecting us in two ways. In a future sense, those who have died believing in Christ will be raised. Even though in John's narrative Jesus has recalled Lazarus back from death, readers of the Gospel know that he will die again.

In a present sense, those who believe in Jesus have available to them a foretaste of resurrection-life in Christ. In John's Gospel this is made clear here by Jesus' radical claim to be the 'resurrection and the life', and by the theme of eternal life (3:16; 20:31; cf. 10:10).

Leader's Notes

For a group to run successfully, it is important that members of the group agree the ground rules. You may want to adopt all or some of the following for your group. Members will contract with each other to make attendance at each of the seven sessions a top priority; members will undertake to prepare for each session by reading through the notes and questions beforehand; anything of a personal nature shared within the group will be treated by the members as confidential; members will respect each other's views, even where they may differ; all members have the right to be listened to with respect.

An important overall aim for the seven sessions looking at the miraculous signs in John's Gospel will be to help the group gain a better understanding of this Gospel, and it is important that members give some time to preparation before each session. As well as the need to understand the text, everyone should be encouraged to look for ways in which it may be applied to their own situation so that, through their study of the seven signs, their Christian lives are enriched.

Leaders should prepare for each session and have some idea of how to allocate the time available to each part of the session. Try to be firm about the time allowed for the Icebreakers, and ensure that the overall atmosphere of the group is friendly and prayerful. There will be times when the group is not able to get through all the questions and leaders need to make a judgment as to when pastoral sensitivity should override the need to include every Discussion Starter.

Gaining familiarity with the text to be studied is an important aim of these sessions. Therefore, following the

Icebreaker for each session, the suggested texts should be read aloud by one or more members of the group. Members who are asked to read should be encouraged to take time to prepare their reading beforehand if possible.

Week 1: The Best is Yet to Come

Opening Icebreaker

As this is the first session, the purpose of this Icebreaker is simply to get people to share something of their experience with the rest of the group whilst, at the same time, getting people to think about their experience of weddings. You will need to watch the time and may want to limit members of the group to two minutes each for this exercise.

At the end of the Icebreaker, focus the group's attention on the Bible study by asking people to close their eyes and listen whilst the leader reads slowly John 1:1–14.

Then begin the session by asking members of the group to read aloud John 2:1–11.

Aim of the Session

The aim of this session is to explore the first miraculous sign performed by Jesus at a social function, amongst many who would already know Him, and especially the way in which the transformation of the water into wine illustrates the effect Jesus can have on the lives of men and women today. In the miracle story, the large stone jars used for ceremonial washing are clearly associated with the old order, but the wine which Jesus gives to replace the water, normally used for purification, represents the new order, characterised by God's grace and the gift of eternal life which Jesus brings into the world.

In Discussion Starter 3, give people time to answer the question in their own way before looking up the relevant verses at the end of the question.

Use Discussion Starter 7 to focus attention back to the key verse of the session (John 1:14) in order to understand how this first sign reflects John's prologue as well as the criteria he uses for selecting the signs included in his Gospel (20:30f.).

Discussion Starter 8 should be used to explore the idea of Jesus offering something new which is better than what has gone before.

Closing Exercise
End this week's session by asking the group to repeat three times to each other, as a closing grace, the words of John 1:14.

Week 2: God's Timing is Perfect

Opening Icebreaker
The purpose of this week's Icebreaker is to help the group get a feel for the drama of the events surrounding and being enacted in this second sign performed by Jesus at Cana. You might want to use a 'dramatised' version of the text and ask group members to read different parts in the story before moving on to the Icebreaker.

The Icebreaker is also to promote empathy with the royal official. As the session progresses, this heightened sense of empathy will help the group to consider how drama and suspense often accompany God's 'perfect' timing, but this is all the more reason for our faith in God to remain firm.

Begin the session by asking members of the group to read aloud John 4:43–54.

Aim of the Session

The overall aim of this week's session is to explore in detail this second miraculous sign performed by Jesus, and to consider how it illustrates the idea of God's perfect timing in the experience of Christians today. Here our supreme example is Jesus who, with His frequent references to His 'hour' in John's Gospel, clearly demonstrates His acute awareness of God's perfect timing.

Discussion Starter 1 links both with the general atmosphere of empathy with characters in the text, encouraged by the Icebreaker, as well as asking people to think seriously about the cost of their own Christian experience as a counterbalance to the joy that comes from experiencing God's perfect timing.

Discussion Starter 3 is not aimed at opening up a discussion which is critical of Christians who do/do not emphasise contemporary signs and wonders. The point is to consider our own attitudes to signs and wonders today in light of Jesus' comments here in John's Gospel. This should be made clear to the group before turning to discussion, and it may be helpful to read Discussion Starters 3 and 4 together before beginning discussion of 3.

Link Discussion Starter 6 with comments made during the Opening Icebreaker.

The primary aim of this session should be brought out firmly through the next two Discussion Starters, and enough time should be allowed for a full discussion.

In Discussion Starter 9, which is focused on 4:53, you may want to link it back to the opening discussion, if appropriate.

Week 3: Healing and Wholeness

Opening Icebreaker

Use this to open up the subject of the confidence we have in Christ and the difference this ought to make to any tendency to procrastinate. There may be some in the group who feel frustrated by their tendency to put things off that they know they ought to do, and yet have not prayerfully considered this in relation to the wholeness Jesus offers to each of us.

Begin the session by asking members of the group to read aloud John 5:1–30.

Aim of the Session

The aim of the session is to focus on the wholeness that can be available through our walk with Christ, wholeness which repairs the damage wrought by broken relationships and other areas of our lives where we feel we have failed. And, especially, it is the wholeness that results when we are open to receive from Jesus His peace as a reality within our innermost beings (cf. John 14:27).

Discussion Starter 1 aims to help the group get a feel for the atmosphere generated by the location of this third sign, before moving on to Discussion Starters 2, 3 and 4 which take us to the heart of the aim for this session.

Explore together, in Discussion Starter 5, the attitudes of Jesus and His opponents to unthinking religious observance before moving the discussion on to consider how these attitudes can affect Christian life today.

Theology is at the heart of Discussion Starter 6. Use the additional verses given to help the group explore the meaning of Jesus' words in verses 19–23.

Use Discussion Starter 8 to think about the current quest for 'spirituality' which marks much of New Age thinking today, before moving on to consider how verse 39 might, in some cases, be the 'other side of the coin'. How can the Church meet the contemporary need for dynamic spiritual life and yet avoid using Scripture in unhelpful ways?

Week 4: Jesus and the Unexpected

Opening Icebreaker

At one level the Icebreaker this week is aimed at the group having fun together. It is intended to be a light-hearted lead into the feeding sign with its multiplication of the loaves and the idea of sharing with others. You should ask for brief, off-the-top-of-their-heads, one sentence responses. At a deeper level, it illustrates the natural generosity of God and His provision for us. After sharing around the group, this latter point should be introduced as a conclusion to the discussion.

Begin the session as usual by asking members of the group to read aloud the texts to be discussed (John 6:1–15, 16–21).

Aim of the Session

This session, together with Week 5, takes a slightly different approach in light of the large amount of text to be covered by the two signs and the important discussion that follows the feeding of the five thousand. In John 6:1–15 we have Jesus' third miraculous sign, the feeding of the crowd in the wilderness, and in 6:16–24 we have the strange story of Jesus walking across the sea which is also recorded by Mark and Matthew. It is only after this incident that John goes on to narrate the significance of the miraculous feeding and what it reveals about Jesus. The overall aim of this session is to look at how Jesus meets our needs. This is aptly demonstrated in terms of meeting physical needs through the story of the miraculous feeding. In John's account of Jesus walking on the water, we see how our emotional needs can be met when we place our trust in Christ during the storms of life. This is demonstrated particularly in 6:21 where John tells us that as soon as the disciples overcame their fear and were willing to allow Jesus to join them, the danger was past and they arrived at their destination.

The first five Discussion Starters are concerned with the feeding of the five thousand. They are designed to help the group dig deeply into the text whilst thinking carefully about issues raised by it for us today.

Using Discussion Starter 5, particularly, give the group time to discuss their experience of God's provision. If you can obtain a copy of George Muller's diary, it might be worth reading an extract illustrating how he experienced God's provision on a daily basis in the Bristol orphanage he ran.[1] (see p.63)

The final three Discussion Starters concentrate on the narrative of Jesus walking on the sea. The Greek text makes it absolutely clear in a number of ways that Jesus actually walked across the sea and renders any attempt to rationalise the miraculous out of this passage futile. In addition to the specific reference to Jesus walking on the water (the Greek word used here, *thalassa* means quite clearly sea, in contrast to land), the disciples' reaction to what they obviously thought was an apparition (cf. Mark 6:49) is typical of being confronted by a divine being or a miraculous event (cf. for example the disciples' reactions to the risen Jesus in the resurrection narratives in Matt. 28:8; Mark 16:6–8; Luke 24:36–42). Seeing Jesus under these circumstances reminded the disciples, His constant companions, to have regard for His heavenly status.

Week 5: Living Bread

Opening Icebreaker

If you have the facility, you might like to begin this session by serving some of your favourite bread before asking members of the group to talk about their favourite bread.

Begin the session by asking members of the group to read aloud John 6:25–70.

Aim of the Session

The overall aim of this session is to consider the implications for us of Jesus' claim to be the bread of life – for each of us as individuals and corporately as the Church.

We focused last week on the ways in which Jesus meets our needs. This week the focus sharpens beyond just meeting our needs, to bread being the sustainer of life itself. In this week's text there is a clear parallel between God's provision in the wilderness during the Exodus and the way this is now superseded by Jesus as the 'bread of life'.

The New Testament writers looked to the Old Testament for 'types', 'examples' or figures that foreshadowed Jesus in some way. For example, in the Gospels, Jesus points to Jonah as foreshadowing His resurrection (Matt. 12:38–42), Paul resorts to typology when he looks to the experience of the Israelites in the wilderness as a foreshadowing of Christian experience (1 Cor. 10:1–5), and the writer to the Hebrews saw the OT priest-king Melchizedek as foreshadowing Jesus in a number of ways (Heb. 7).

The point of Discussion Starter 2 is to offer an opportunity for the group to share how you all spend, or struggle with (!) your quiet times. This should not be seen as threatening, but rather as an opportunity to learn from one another. As the leader you may want to begin the discussion by sharing something of your own experience of the joys and difficulties of finding time to be with God on a regular basis, and how this has affected your own Christian journey. It may be appropriate to have some material handy that deals with spending daily time with God – some Bible devotional notes for example, that the group members can browse through later.

In Discussion Starter 3, it is important not to ignore the relevance, for the narrative as a whole and Jesus' claim to be the bread of life in particular, of the Old Testament traditions which form the background to what Jesus is saying here. The comparison is between the old order, where the manna in the desert had a temporary effect, and the new order, where the sustenance that Jesus offers leads to eternal life.

John's Gospel does not contain the words of institution – where Jesus takes the bread and the wine during the last supper with His disciples and tells them to eat and drink as a memorial to Him (Mark 14:22–25; Matt. 26:26–30; Luke 22:14–23) – and yet it seems clear that Jesus' words in verses 51–58 assume knowledge of them. Discussion Starter 6 provides an opportunity to discuss Jesus' words, and for everyone to share their understanding of the Eucharist and the part it plays corporately and individually for them.

The last two Discussion Starters are designed to promote reflection about what makes it hard to be a Christian today and how, along with Peter, knowing who Jesus is and what He has done helps Christians overcome these hardships.

Week 6: Amazing Grace

Opening Icebreaker

This week's Icebreaker should prove amusing. My younger daughter, who now has children of her own, was so surprised to find herself saying things to her own children that her mother had said to her that she picked up the telephone immediately and told us that not only did she find herself saying the same things, but she actually sounded like her mother!

Begin the session by asking members of the group to read aloud John 9:1–41.

Aim of the Session

The focus for this week's session is 'amazing grace'. The former blind man's words in John 9:25, 'I was blind but now I see', remind us of the words of John Newton's hymn and reflect both the experience of the man healed by Jesus in the story as well as the experience of Christians down the ages.

At each stage in the story, Jesus provides us with a model of grace in action. The healing of the blind man acts as a sign that provides graphic validation of Jesus' claim to be the light of the world. Rather than condemn the man for sin, as popular opinion expressed by the disciples appeared to do, Jesus graciously meets the man's deepest need. When, as a result of his healing, the man is victimised by Jesus' opponents, Jesus graciously seeks him out and restores to him his sense of being accepted by God.

The final Discussion Starter is intended to enable the group to consider what it means to be the people of God, and how the model provided by Jesus in this story illustrates how the Church as the people of God should be characterised by the gracious way it acts towards others. 'The Rule of St. Benedict', written for monks in the sixth century (and which would have been followed by the monks living for many years at Waverley Abbey, next to the home of CWR), advocates that Christians treat friend and stranger alike as though the other person were Christ. Benedict writes: 'All guests who present themselves are to be welcomed as Christ who said: "I was a stranger and you welcomed me" (Matt. 25:35).'

Discussion Starter 1 provides an opportunity for the group to discuss both the idea of being responsible for our own wrongdoing, and the relationship between sin and physical consequences. The group may want to widen the discussion to consider how these issues may be relevant, for example in the spread of the worldwide AIDS epidemic.

Discussion Starters 3 and 4 will need to be handled sensitively, but by now there should be a strong enough sense of trust within the group for you all to feel able to share at this level.

Week 7: Death Loses its Sting

Opening Icebreaker

Ask the group members to pair up and share their response to the Icebreaker with each other. Make it clear that, like other personal information shared within the group, anything they discuss here should be treated as strictly confidential and must remain within the group. This Icebreaker may bring unresolved hurts to the surface, and for this reason it is suggested that the group be led in a prayer of forgiveness, letting go of past hurts, real or imaginary. Allow several minutes for sharing before ending this part of the session with the prayer of forgiveness.

Begin the session by asking members of the group to read aloud John 11:1–44. Follow this by a short period of silence before other members of the group read aloud the verses from Paul's letter to the Corinthians (1 Cor. 15:1–58).

Aim of the Session

The aim of this final session is to understand something of the tension – the 'now' and 'not yet' – we encounter in the New Testament's teaching about resurrection; what Jesus meant by His claim to be the resurrection and the life, and what this means for us today.

In 1 Corinthians 15, Paul argues for the centrality of the resurrection for the Christian gospel. First he deals with the historical reality of the resurrection and the fact that the risen Jesus was seen by many early believers. Having established the fact of Jesus' resurrection, Paul then points out that its significance for the Church lies in the fact that Jesus' resurrection was a precursor, or firstfruits, for what all Christians may hope for in Christ.

But the resurrection is not just about post-mortem existence. It guarantees the truth of the Christian message that through His death Jesus has dealt with the roots of humanity's alienation from God, resulting in judgment, and made reconciliation with a loving heavenly Father a reality for all who by faith would claim it.

As Jesus put it here: 'I am the resurrection and the life. He who believes in me will live, even though he dies; and whoever lives and believes in me will never die' (John 11:25–26). In our passage, Jesus then puts a crucial question to Martha and, by extension, addresses the same question to Christians in every generation: 'Do you believe this?' For all who can answer in the affirmative, we can say, with Paul, that death has truly lost its sting.

The Discussion Starters for this seventh session are all quite straightforward, with the final one giving the opportunity for the group to consider how their understanding of John's Gospel may have changed as a result of their study of the seven signs recorded by him.

Note

1. CWR has published a beautifully illustrated book recounting the life of George Muller, with insights into his prayer life: *Robber of the Cruel Streets* by Clive Langmead. A docu-drama on DVD is also available.

Notes...

Be inspired by God.
Every day.

COVER TO COVER | EVERY **DAY** JAN/FEB 2017

Genesis 12–50
John 12–21

Bringing you deeper biblical understanding **CWR**

Cover to Cover Every Day

In-depth study of the Bible, book by book. Part of a five-year series. Available as an email subscription or on eBook and Kindle.

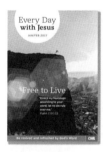

Every Day with Jesus

The popular daily Bible reading notes by Selwyn Hughes.

Inspiring Women Every Day

Daily insight and encouragement written by women for women.

Life Every Day

Lively Bible notes, with Jeff Lucas' wit and wisdom.

To order or subscribe, visit **www.cwr.org.uk/store** or call **01252 784700**.
Also available in Christian bookshops.

 Print subscription available

 **Large Print subscription** available

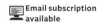 **Email subscription** available

The bestselling *Cover to Cover* Bible Study Series

1 Corinthians
Growing a Spirit-filled church
ISBN: 978-1-85345-374-8

2 Corinthians
Restoring harmony
ISBN: 978-1-85345-551-3

1 Peter
Good reasons for hope
ISBN: 978-1-78259-088-0

2 Peter
Living in the light of God's promises
ISBN: 978-1-78259-403-1

1 Timothy
*Healthy churches –
effective Christians*
ISBN: 978-1-85345-291-8

23rd Psalm
The Lord is my shepherd
ISBN: 978-1-85345-449-3

2 Timothy and Titus
Vital Christianity
ISBN: 978-1-85345-338-0

Abraham
Adventures of faith
ISBN: 978-1-78259-089-7

Acts 1–12
Church on the move
ISBN: 978-1-85345-574-2

Acts 13–28
To the ends of the earth
ISBN: 978-1-85345-592-6

Barnabas
Son of encouragement
ISBN: 978-1-85345-911-5

Bible Genres
Hearing what the Bible really says
ISBN: 978-1-85345-987-0

Daniel
Living boldly for God
ISBN: 978-1-85345-986-3

David
A man after God's own heart
ISBN: 978-1-78259-444-4

Ecclesiastes
*Hard questions and
spiritual answers*
ISBN: 978-1-85345-371-7

Elijah
A man and his God
ISBN: 978-1-85345-575-9

Elisha
A lesson in faithfulness
ISBN: 978-1-78259-494-9

Ephesians
Claiming your inheritance
ISBN: 978-1-85345-229-1

Esther
For such a time as this
ISBN: 978-1-85345-511-7

Fruit of the Spirit
Growing more like Jesus
ISBN: 978-1-85345-375-5

Galatians
Freedom in Christ
ISBN: 978-1-85345-648-0

God's Rescue Plan
*Finding God's fingerprints
on human history*
ISBN: 978-1-85345-294-9

Great Prayers of the Bible
Applying them to our lives today
ISBN: 978-1-85345-253-6

Hebrews
Jesus – simply the best
ISBN: 978-1-85345-337-3

Hosea
The love that never fails
ISBN: 978-1-85345-290-1

Isaiah 1-39
Prophet to the nations
ISBN: 978-1-85345-510-0

Isaiah 40-66
Prophet of restoration
ISBN: 978-1-85345-550-6

James
Faith in action
ISBN: 978-1-85345-293-2

Jeremiah
The passionate prophet
ISBN: 978-1-85345-372-4

John's Gospel
Exploring the seven miraculous signs
ISBN: 978-1-85345-295-6

Joseph
The power of forgiveness and reconciliation
ISBN: 978-1-85345-252-9

Joshua 1-10
Hand in hand with God
ISBN: 978-1-78259-542-7

Judges 1-8
The spiral of faith
ISBN: 978-1-85345-681-7

Judges 9-21
Learning to live God's way
ISBN: 978-1-85345-910-8

Luke
A prescription for living
ISBN: 978-1-78259-270-9

Mark
Life as it is meant to be lived
ISBN: 978-1-85345-233-8

Mary
The mother of Jesus
ISBN: 978-1-78259-402-4

Moses
Face to face with God
ISBN: 978-1-85345-336-6

Names of God
Exploring the depths of God's character
ISBN: 978-1-85345-680-0

Nehemiah
Principles for life
ISBN: 978-1-85345-335-9

Parables
Communicating God on earth
ISBN: 978-1-85345-340-3

Philemon
From slavery to freedom
ISBN: 978-1-85345-453-0

Philippians
Living for the sake of the gospel
ISBN: 978-1-85345-421-9

Prayers of Jesus
Hearing His heartbeat
ISBN: 978-1-85345-647-3

Proverbs
Living a life of wisdom
ISBN: 978-1-85345-373-1

Revelation 1-3
Christ's call to the Church
ISBN: 978-1-85345-461-5

Revelation 4-22
The Lamb wins! Christ's final victory
ISBN: 978-1-85345-411-0

Rivers of Justice
Responding to God's call to righteousness today
ISBN: 978-1-85345-339-7

Ruth
Loving kindness in action
ISBN: 978-1-85345-231-4

The Armour of God
Living in His strength
ISBN: 978-1-78259-583-0

The Beatitudes
Immersed in the grace of Christ
ISBN: 978-1-78259-495-6

The Covenants
God's promises and their relevance today
ISBN: 978-1-85345-255-0

The Creed
Belief in action
ISBN: 978-1-78259-202-0

The Divine Blueprint
God's extraordinary power in ordinary lives
ISBN: 978-1-85345-292-5

The Holy Spirit
Understanding and experiencing Him
ISBN: 978-1-85345-254-3

The Image of God
His attributes and character
ISBN: 978-1-85345-228-4

The Kingdom
Studies from Matthew's Gospel
ISBN: 978-1-85345-251-2

The Letter to the Romans
Good news for everyone
ISBN: 978-1-85345-250-5

The Lord's Prayer
Praying Jesus' way
ISBN: 978-1-85345-460-8

The Prodigal Son
Amazing grace
ISBN: 978-1-85345-412-7

The Second Coming
Living in the light of Jesus' return
ISBN: 978-1-85345-422-6

The Sermon on the Mount
Life within the new covenant
ISBN: 978-1-85345-370-0

Thessalonians
Building Church in changing times
ISBN: 978-1-78259-443-7

The Ten Commandments
Living God's Way
ISBN: 978-1-85345-593-3

The Uniqueness of our Faith
What makes Christianity distinctive?
ISBN: 978-1-85345-232-1

For current prices or to order, visit **www.cwr.org.uk/store**
Available online or from Christian bookshops.

SmallGroup central

All of our small group ideas and resources in one place

Online:

www.smallgroupcentral.org.uk
is filled with free video teaching,
tools, articles and a whole host
of ideas.

On the road:

A range of seminars themed for
small groups can be brought to
your local community. Contact us at
hello@smallgroupcentral.org.uk

In print:

Books, study guides and DVDs
covering an extensive list of themes,
Bible books and life issues.

Log on and find out more at:
www.smallgroupcentral.org.uk

Courses and events

Waverley Abbey College

Publishing and media

Conference facilities

Transforming lives

CWR's vision is to enable people to experience personal transformation through applying God's Word to their lives and relationships.

Our Bible-based training and resources help people around the world to:
• Grow in their walk with God
• Understand and apply Scripture to their lives
• Resource themselves and their church
• Develop pastoral care and counselling skills
• Train for leadership
• Strengthen relationships, marriage and family life and much more.

Our insightful writers provide daily Bible reading notes and other resources for all ages, and our experienced course designers and presenters have gained an international reputation for excellence and effectiveness.

CWR's Training and Conference Centres in Surrey and East Sussex, England, provide excellent facilities in idyllic settings – ideal for both learning and spiritual refreshment.

CWR Applying God's Word
to everyday life and relationships

CWR, Waverley Abbey House,
Waverley Lane, Farnham,
Surrey GU9 8EP, UK

Telephone: **+44 (0)1252 784700**
Email: **info@cwr.org.uk**
Website: **www.cwr.org.uk**

Registered Charity No. 294387
Company Registration No. 1990308